'ABDU'L-BAHÁ
THE MASTER

'ABDU'L-BAHÁ

'ABDU'L-BAHÁ
THE MASTER

a compilation from the
writings of
GEORGE TOWNSHEND
Hand of the Cause of God

*(Sometime Canon of St Patrick's Cathedral,
Dublin, Archdeacon of Clonfert)*

with a Foreword and annotations
by
DAVID HOFMAN

GEORGE RONALD
OXFORD

GEORGE RONALD, *Publisher*
Oxford
www.grbooks.com

This compilation and notes © DAVID HOFMAN 1987
Original texts © GEORGE TOWNSHEND 1957
All Rights Reserved

First published in hardcover 1987
Softcover edition 2020

ISBN 978-0-85398-254-8

*A catalogue record for this book is available
from the British Library*

CONTENTS

Foreword	1
The Tablets of 'Abdu'l-Bahá to George Townshend	5
The Exemplar	15
The Master	23
A Study of a Christlike Character	37
The Letters of 'Abdu'l-Bahá	51
The Fire of the King's Love	69
Further Reading	77

'But for my part, I fell head over heels in love with 'Abdu'l-Bahá's words when first I read them in print and I have been getting deeper and deeper in all these years. And I shall never get out!'
Letter to Bernard Leach, 1954

FOREWORD

The Hand of the Cause of God George Townshend was designated by Shoghi Effendi, Guardian of the Bahá'í Faith, as '. . . the best writer we have . . . the pre-eminent Bahá'í writer.' His major works are in print, in several languages, but his many essays and shorter works are available only in out-of-print pamphlets, the volumes of *The Bahá'í World,* early copies of Bahá'í magazines and as Introductions to basic Bahá'í books, notably *God Passes By* and *The Dawn-Breakers.* While a large compilation of his poems and essays, meditations and other literary pieces is planned, it seems both felicitous and timely to assemble his particular writings about 'Abdu'l-Bahá in one separate volume. In this way his own portrait of the Master emerges, with befitting reverence to the Centre of the Covenant, the Exemplar, the Mystery of God.

The former Archdeacon of Clonfert was fully aware of the specific call made by Bahá'u'lláh upon the Christian West to arise and take the lead in promoting the unity of the human race and the establishment of the long-awaited, Christ-promised Kingdom of God on earth. In his manifesto, addressed to all Christians everywhere, penned after his renunciation of his Orders and ecclesiastical offices, he recalled Bahá'u'lláh's addresses to the monarchs of Europe, the Pope, the 'Rulers of America and the Presidents of the Republics therein', the bishops, clergy and various churches of Christendom; and he urged them to recognise Christ returned, in the glory of the Father, with the principles, laws and spiritual teachings for the complete fulfilment of His prayer and promise made two thousand years earlier.

He dwells with emphasis and in detail on 'Abdu'l-Bahá's historic journeys to the West, immediately after His release from prison in 1908. From the Holy Land to Geneva, London and Paris; throughout North America to the western outpost of San Francisco and back again to England and continental Europe, He proclaimed the message of God as it had never before in history been proclaimed. In doing so, He revealed Himself as the true lover of humanity, the moon to the sun of Bahá'u'lláh's revelation, the uplifter, encourager, hope-bringer, healer, forgiver and concealer of sins, the shepherd, protector and guide of a humanity gone far astray. Only too well He knew the reality of the feet of clay with which Western civilization so arrogantly bestrode the world, and its approaching doom. But far from dwelling on their weaknesses and omissions He called men to their higher capabilities, opened new horizons of spiritual wonder to their earth-bound vision, upheld and showed the practicality of their traditional, forgotten ideals and presented a prospect of a world so enthralling, so radiant, so vibrant with happiness and well-being as only God could establish. And this, He told them, was God's purpose and the mission of Bahá'u'lláh. And the time is now.

In describing all this, George Townshend presents a picture of 'Abdu'l-Bahá which answers modern man's hunger for Divine love and his search for his own soul.

No apology is made for including in this pastiche of 'Abdu'l-Bahá the correspondence between Him and George Townshend. The items are fully as revealing of 'Abdu'l-Bahá as they are of their beatified recipient, in whose life they were, without any doubt whatsoever, and beyond all comparison, the supreme influence.

David Hofman
Haifa, 1987

THE TABLETS FROM 'ABDU'L-BAHÁ TO GEORGE TOWNSHEND

A full account of the circumstances surrounding the receipt of the two Tablets from 'Abdu'l-Bahá, with detailed commentary on their contents, is given in chapter 5 of *George Townshend* (Oxford: George Ronald, 1983). The Tablets were written as part of a correspondence initiated by George Townshend. Translations of both accompanied the originals, the first being by 'Abdu'l-Bahá's grandson, Shoghi Effendi, later to become 'Abdu'l-Bahá's successor and Guardian of the Bahá'í Faith; the second was made by Luṭfu'lláh Ḥakím, a distinguished early believer, who became one of the first nine members of the Universal House of Justice. The translations are printed as received. George Townshend's reply to the second Tablet (entitled by him *Surrender*) arrived in Haifa ten days after 'Abdu'l-Bahá's ascension. The interested reader is referred to the above-mentioned biography.

LETTER FROM GEORGE TOWNSHEND TO 'ABDU'L-BAHÁ
10 JUNE 1919

Dear Abdul Baha,

I am impelled to send you a letter, asking Mr Remey of America to forward it to you since I do not know your direction. I want to acknowledge the light and uplift and happiness and exhilaration which are coming to me through the knowledge of your teachings, the reports of your life and through the writings of Bahaollah; and to offer my thanks, deep heartfelt and ever-growing for this extraordinary benefit.

Recognizing that you are immersed in cares and important work, I should hardly have ventured to intrude upon you but that I read in Vol. ii of your Tablets the other day that it is necessary for every soul who believes in [his] Lord to send Abdul Baha a letter of acknowledgement in the Oneness of God.

Already I have tried to communicate with you sending out a spiritual message and trusting that through the operation of the universal consciousness the call of my heart would reach you across lands and seas. I wished to thank you and to ask you for help that I might make the better speed out of the Valley of Search into the Valley of Love. I am not impatient; not a bit! I am quite willing to travel for the hundred thousand years,* – but I am hungry and empty! I lived in America for nearly 13 years, working at first as a

---

* *The steed of this Valley is patience; without patience the wayfarer on this journey will reach nowhere and attain no goal. Nor should he ever be downhearted; if he strive for a hundred thousand years and yet fail to behold the beauty of the Friend, he should not falter.* Bahá'u'lláh, The Valley of Search from *The Seven Valleys*.

missionary in Utah; then I became connected with an ethical movement called The Great Work, abandoned the ministry for it, believing it better and more sincere than the Church, and became at once involved in all sorts of hardships including neuritis which afflicted eyes and arms so that I could neither read nor write. But I never for an instant regretted what I had done, and in spite of my handicaps I held a professorship of English in the University of the South, Tennessee. In the spring of 1916 a remarkable spiritual intimation came to me, without sight or sound or any appeal to the senses, but overwhelming in its power, of a complete change at hand: something happy and wonderful but otherwise quite indefinite. In June 1916 I learned in one moment the Movement for which I had done so much was based on fraud. I came home to my people in Ireland, returned to the ministry of the Church I was born and bred in; and then in the winter of 1916 I was brought into touch with Bahaism by an American friend, Miss Louise Finley, of Sewanee, Tennessee, (herself not a believer – as yet).

From that hour to this I have read and studied the Bahai books and used the Bahai prayers, and found there a light and exaltation and spirit of triumph which fill me with joy and enthral me and carry me on to seek and seek. Every morning now I rise early to give the first hour of the day, the most precious of all, to prayer and meditation. The consciousness of the Great Presence has already begun to dawn on me and I live now in a new world, awestruck, wondering, humble and uplifted, and wishing eternally for more light in my darkness and more strength in my weakness. I have recently married and my wife by her example is the best as well as the dearest of my near-by teachers. I never was so happy – I never was happy at all, but I will be happier yet! I want so much to win out of the thraldom of self and error and this blindness and ignorance. I am able to read and write again, and I read nothing but the work of regenerate souls, Bahai writings and the Bible and Tagore: I could learn little from others as ignorant as I! Help me a little if you have time to remember the least of all strugglers. And let my last word be – from my heart and soul all *thanks* and *blessing*!

       Yours
       George Townshend

THE FIRST TABLET FROM ʿABDUʾL-BAHÁ
24 JULY 1919

To his honor Mr. George Townshend, Galway, Ireland: Upon him be greeting and praise.

He is God

O Thou who art thirsty for the Fountain of Truth!

Thy letter was received and the account of thy life has been known. Praise be to God thou hast ever, like unto the nightingale, sought the Divine rose-garden and like unto the verdure of the Meadow yearned for the out-pourings of the cloud of guidance. That is why thou hast been transferred from one condition to another until ultimately thou hast attained unto the fountain of Truth, hast illumined thy sight, hast revived and animated thy heart, hast chanted the verses of guidance and hast turned thy face toward the enkindled fire on the Mount of Sinai.

At present, I pray on thy behalf that the fire of love be set aglow in thy heart and spiritual sensations may stir and move thy soul, so that thou mayest be quickened, mayest fly and soar toward the Ideal Friend, mayest sacrifice thy soul to the Beloved of the World and consecrate thy life to the diffusion of the Divine Fragrances. If thou attainest unto such a bounty thou shalt become the sign of guidance, shalt become an enkindled candle in the gathering of men, shalt be baptized with the spirit of life and the fire of the Love of God, shalt be born again from the world of nature and shalt attain unto everlasting life.

Upon thee be Bahaʾil Abha.

(Sgd.) abdul Baha abbas

GEORGE TOWNSHEND'S REPLY TO THE FIRST TABLET

Recognition

Hail to Thee, Scion of Glory, Whose utterance poureth abroad
The joy of the heavenly knowledge and the light of the greatest of days!
Poet of mysteries chanting in rapture the beauty of God,
   Unto Thee be thanksgiving and praise!

Child of the darkness that wandered in gloom but dreamed of the light,
Lo! I have seen Thy splendour ablaze in the heavens afar
Showering gladness and glory and shattering the shadows of night,
   And seen no other star.

Thy words are to me as fragrances borne from the garden of heaven,
Beams of a lamp that is hid in the height of a holier world,
Arrows of fire that pierce and destroy with the might of the levin
   Into our midnight hurled.

Sword of the Father! none other can rend the dark veil from my eyes,
None other can beat from my limbs with the shearing blade of God's might

The sins I am fettered withal and give me the power to rise
  And come forth to the fullness of light.

Lo! Thou hast breathed on my sorrow the sweetness of faith and of hope,
Thou hast chanted high paeans of joy that my heart's echoes ever repeat,
And the path to the knowledge of God begins to glimmer and ope
  Before my faltering feet.

Weak and unworthy my praise. Yet, as from its throbbing throat
Some lone bird pours its song to the flaming infinite sky,
So unto Thee in the zenith I lift from a depth remote
  This broken human cry.

THE SECOND TABLET FROM 'ABDU'L-BAHÁ
19 DECEMBER 1920

His honour Rev. George Townshend, Ireland:
Unto him be Baha'u'llah-el Abha!

He is God!
O Thou illumined heavenly soul and revered personage in the Kingdom!

Thy letter has been received. Every word indicated the progress and upliftment of thy spirit and conscience. These heavenly susceptibilities of thine form a magnet which attracts the confirmation of the Kingdom of God; and so the doors of realities and meanings will be open unto thee, and the confirmations of the Kingdom of God will envelop thee.

The heart of man is like unto a nest, and the Teachings of His Holiness Baha'u'llah like unto a sweet singing bird. Unquestionably from this nest the melody of the Kingdom will be transmitted to the ears, bestowing heavenly susceptibilities upon the souls and quickening upon the spirits.

It is my hope that thy church will come under the Heavenly Jerusalem.

Do not mind the weakness of thy physical limbs! Praise be to God thy spirit is full of vigour. His Holiness Christ says that the body is weak and grieved, but the spirit is in the greatest joy. Then know thou that through this very spirit thy body will be strengthened! Be assured thou art under the favours of His Holiness Baha'u'llah!

Convey on my behalf greeting and respect to my dear daughter thy revered wife, and other members of thy family.
Unto thee be the Glory of Abha!
(Sgd.) abdul Baha abbas

GEORGE TOWNSHEND'S REPLY
TO THE SECOND TABLET

Surrender

To 'Abdu'l-Bahá,
Haifa, Palestine.

O Holy One who dwellest in the remote heaven and heaven of heavens!
Master of the will of the world, Director of Destiny,
The One Hope of all Humanity,
My Desired One, the Conqueror of my Heart, Teacher and Guide!
As the dark earth moves into the light of the sun,
as Error turns to Truth, Ignorance to Knowledge, weakness to strength, so do I now address myself to thee.

The Truth which thou hast spoken has enveloped and consumed me. I have no thought nor hope nor longing other than this.

It illumines the Past, makes clear the Present, bestows hope for the Future. Where the rays of this Sun fall, there is Beauty and Love, Wisdom and Gladness; beyond lies a wilderness, a desert, the haunt of despair, horrible, detestable.

To the Truth which thou dost reveal, to the divine Love which thou dost dispense, to the Hidden Mystery which is in thy keeping, I offer and resign myself wholly and utterly, to be its witness, its soldier, its thrall, seeking nothing else, knowing nothing else, though deserving nothing here or hereafter.

Freely, willingly, with a song of exultation in my heart and blessings on my lips, I make this surrender. I cannot live nor exist and do otherwise than thus yield myself. That from which I flee is no longer tolerable. That to which I turn is the reality, the inborn Truth of all men and of the world as of me.

My submission has to be. It is part of the nature of things, of the order of the Universe. Aught less would be misery and death.

Of earthly perplexities I say nothing. I cannot tell what may be my field of labour or the manner of my witness – whether I am to remain as I now am seeking to find and to proclaim the veritable Christ or to chant in fuller tones the Day of God from some unfaded Tree.

This one thing I ask: that I may have the wisdom to understand and the firmness to obey implicitly the command of God.

A creature of Time, a child of Error, helpless and impotent, I bow before thee and the Eternal Truth which shines through thee and here commit myself utterly and for ever to the good pleasure of God.

That mercy which I crave for myself I crave for those too whom the bounty of God has given me, my wife, my little son, my little daughter.

Praise and thanksgiving be unto thee, O mighty glorious inscrutable Lord of Forgiveness and Love, Who hast guided the feet of this wanderer to the highway of the Kingdom.

Thy Servant and Suppliant
George Townshend

THE EXEMPLAR

This chapter is taken from one of George Townshend's major works, *The Promise of All Ages* (Oxford: George Ronald, rev. edn 1948). The passages appear towards the end of Chapter IX of that book. In it 'Abdu'l-Bahá is portrayed as the Exemplar of the true life of man, treading the mystic path with practical feet, as was said of Him, overcoming enmity with love, responding to injury with love, returning love for hatred, for chains and imprisonment, acting always with love, caring for the poor, the sick, the bereaved, the misfits and outcasts, walking with kings to their benefit, dispensing love and encouragement, happiness and love, love and more love.

George concludes his chapter, 'This love now pouring down from God in fullest measure upon the awakening consciousness of mankind is the power that will regenerate human nature, and will create in deed and in fact a new heaven and a new earth.'

'Abbás Effendi, born the heir to high distinction and to wide estates, at the age of nine years followed His father into exile, and from that moment to His death at an advanced age made Himself as nothing but the servant of the Great Beloved, and counted His title 'Abdu'l-Bahá, 'the Bondservant of Glory', as His sword and His crown.

In the well-known photographs taken in Paris, strength of intellect and will appear in harmony with a great humility and the sadness of a heart that ached in sympathy with a suffering world.

Only one European is known to have written an account of an interview with the Báb; only one likewise to have recorded an interview with Bahá'u'lláh. But many travellers and pilgrims from the West visited 'Abdu'l-Bahá in His home in Palestine and testified to the warmth and the breadth of His sympathy, His kindness and His charm.

When in His old age, broken in health, He visited the West in an effort to deter men from the war He saw impending, thousands of people in Germany, France, England and America saw Him and heard Him speak. His genial manner, His quick sympathy, His ever-flowing kindliness, His selfless devotion to the Cause of His Father, were evident to all who had the privilege of meeting Him. Physically exhausted, He never declined an opportunity of giving His message. *Where there is love*, He would say, *effort is a rest*. There are still many in the Occident as well as in the Orient who testify to the power of an utterance which touched all hearts and brought to every attentive ear a new knowledge of what is meant by true goodwill and love.

> All the people know him and love him – the rich and the poor, the young and the old – even the babe leaping in its mother's arms. If he hears of anyone sick in the city – Moslem or Christian, or of any other sect, it matters not – he is each day at their bedside or sends a trusty messenger . . . He claims nothing for himself – neither comfort, nor honour, nor repose. Three or four hours of sleep suffice him; all the remainder of his time and strength are given to the succour of those who suffer in spirit or in body.

So wrote M. H. Phelps in his *Abbas Effendi* (1903).

Another, who knew 'Abdu'l-Bahá (the Governor of Haifa) spoke of Him as follows (*The Passing of 'Abdu'l-Bahá*, p. 22):

> Most of us here have, I think, a clear picture of Sir 'Abdu'l-Bahá Abbas, of his dignified figure walking thoughtfully in our streets, of his courteous and gracious manner, of his kindness, of his love for little children and flowers, of his generosity and care for the poor and suffering. So gentle was he, and so simple, that in his presence one almost forgot that he was also a great teacher, and that his writings and conversations have been a solace and an inspiration to hundreds and thousands of people in the East and in the West.

An American meeting 'Abdu'l-Bahá in Thonon recorded his experience as follows:

> To look upon so wonderful a human being, to respond utterly to the charm of his presence – this brought me continual happiness . . . Patriarchal, majestic, strong, yet infinitely kind, he appeared like some just king that very moment descended from his throne to mingle with a devoted people . . . He laughed heartily from time to time – indeed, the idea of asceticism or useless misery of any kind cannot attach itself to this fully-developed personality. The divine element in him does not feed at the expense of the human element, but appears rather to vitalise and enrich the human element by its own abundance, as if he had attained his spiritual development by fulfilling his social relations with the utmost ardour (Horace Holley, *Bahaism: The Modern Social Religion*, pp. 213–14).

Of His visit to London, it was written (*'Abdu'l-Bahá in London*, pp. xiii and xiv):

> A profound impression remained in the minds and memories of all sorts and conditions of men and women. The width of 'Abdu'l-Bahá's sympathy proved, in every instance, as helpful as his discrimination and perspicacity in dealing with difficulties whether subtle or obvious. Each person approaching him found himself understood, and was astonished and relieved by 'Abdu'l-Bahá's comprehension of religious differences; above all, of religious agree-

ments . . . He left behind him many friends. His love had kindled love. His heart had opened to the West, and the West had closed around this patriarchal presence from the East.

When in November 1921 'Abdu'l-Bahá passed away, one of the tributes paid to him included these words:

> The eyes that had always looked out with loving-kindness upon humanity, whether friends or foes, were now closed. The hands that had ever been stretched forth to give alms to the poor and needy, the halt and the maimed, the blind, the orphan and the widow, had now finished their labour. The feet that with untiring zeal had gone upon the ceaseless errands of the Lord of Compassion were now at rest. The lips that had so eloquently championed the cause of the suffering sons of men, were now hushed in silence. The heart that had so powerfully throbbed with wondrous love for the children of God was now stilled. His glorious spirit had passed from the life of earth, from the persecutions of the enemies of righteousness, from the storm and stress of well-nigh eighty years of indefatigable toil for the good of others (*The Passing of 'Abdu'l-Bahá*, pp. 9–10).

These quotations, culled almost at random, suggest something of the impression made on those Westerners who met and knew Him. The classic expression of the inspiring power which He could impart to one prepared to receive it is from the pen of one of the writers cited above.

. . . As the party rose I saw among them a stately old man, robed in a cream-coloured gown, his white hair and beard shining in the sun. He displayed a beauty of stature, an inevitable harmony of attitude and dress I had never seen nor thought of in men. Without having ever visualised the Master, I knew that this was he. My whole body underwent a shock. My heart leaped, my knees weakened, a thrill of acute receptive feeling flowed from head to foot. I seemed to have turned into some most sensitive sense-organ, as if eyes and ears were not enough for this sublime impression. In every part of me I stood aware of 'Abdu'l-Bahá's presence. From sheer happiness I wanted to cry – it seemed the most suitable form of self-expression at my command. While my own personality was flowing away, even while I exhibited a state of complete humility, a new being, not my own, assumed its place. A glory, as it were from the summits of human nature, poured into me, and I was conscious of a most intense impulse to admire. In 'Abdu'l-Bahá I felt the awful presence of Bahá'u'lláh, and as my thoughts returned to activity, I realised that I had drawn as near as man now may to pure spirit and pure being. This wonderful experience came to me beyond my own volition. I had entered the Master's presence and become the servant of a higher will for its own purpose. Even my memory of that temporary change of being bears strange authority over me. I know what men can become; and that single overcharged moment, shining out from the dark mountain pass of all past time, reflects like a mirror I can turn upon all circumstances to consider their worth by an intelligence purer than my own (*Modern Social Religion*, Appendix I, pp. 211, 212).

THE MASTER

This is chapter 14 of *Christ and Bahá'u'lláh*, designated by Shoghi Effendi as George Townshend's 'crowning achievement'. Here we see 'Abdu'l-Bahá in action, carrying the Message of the new Day to the western world, giving His first public address to an overflowing congregation in City Temple, London, uplifting hearts with the assured vision of a new era for mankind.

Throughout Europe and North America He addressed audiences of varied types and interests, always encouraging, assuring, arousing latent capacities for spiritual awareness and growth. People flocked to hear Him, surrounded Him, plied Him with questions, basked in the sunshine of His good humour, love and inspiration.

Bahá'u'lláh appointed in His written Will His son 'Abdu'l-Bahá as His successor and with this successorship joined powers to which no successor of any earlier Prophet had attained and which give 'Abdu'l-Bahá a position altogether unique in religious history. Bahá'u'lláh designated Him as the Centre and pivot of His peerless Covenant; as the perfect mirror of His life, to exemplify His teachings; as the unerring interpreter of His Word; as the embodiment of every Bahá'í ideal and virtue.

Bahá'u'lláh called Him the Mystery of God and wrote further of Him,

> *a Word hath, as a token of Our grace, gone forth from the Most Great Tablet – a Word which God hath adorned with the ornament of His own Self, and made it sovereign over the earth and all that is therein, and a sign of His greatness and power among its people ... Render thanks unto God, O people, for His appearance; for verily He is the most great Favour unto you, the most perfect bounty upon you; and through Him every mouldering bone is quickened.**

Such was He who was now to give a large part of His time and effort to the service of the Christian West.

'Abdu'l-Bahá was the age-fellow of the Bahá'í Faith; He had been born on the same evening as the Declaration of the Báb; had been the first to recognize, at the

---
* *Súriy-i-Ghusn* (Tablet of the Branch)

age of nine, the exalted transformation of Bahá'u'lláh after His Call, and had gone at the same time into exile with His Father. In 1868 He entered with His Father the Most Great Prison of 'Akká, remaining in captivity for forty years till the Young Turk Revolution in the year 1908 gave Him His liberty. In 1910, although in poor health owing to His prison suffering, He set out to visit the West, and made two tours occupying three years. His chief addresses given at this time are recorded in *The Promulgation of Universal Peace* (Talks in America), *Paris Talks* and *'Abdu'l-Bahá in London*.

As He knew well, the position of the West at this time was already one of great danger, although the Christians of the West had no idea whatever of the retribution that was confronting them. 'Abdu'l-Bahá has briefly explained what had happened in one of His Tablets which begins with the following lines:

> *O Army of Life! East and West have joined to worship stars of faded splendour, and have turned in prayer unto darkened horizons. Both have utterly neglected the broad foundation of God's sacred laws, and have grown unmindful of the merits and virtues of His religion. They have regarded certain customs and conventions as the basis of the Divine faith, and have firmly established themselves therein. They have imagined themselves as having attained a glorious pinnacle of achievement and prosperity, when in reality they have touched the innermost depths of heedlessness and deprived themselves wholly of God's bounteous gifts.**

---

* *Bahá'í Scripture*, p. 331.

The people of Europe and America whom He addressed were not only completely oblivious of their real condition as seen by Him, but held the very opposite opinion. They were assured that the great and mighty civilization of the Christian West was due to their own effort, and that it was the final product of all civilizations of the past, of the Greek and Roman and that of Persia and India and China and Egypt, which had been preparatory only. They had no doubt that they at this time were the most enlightened generation of the most enlightened age the world had ever known. Physical science had, they thought, reached the limit of reality and probed all the problems and in fact knew all that was to be known. White man in the plenitude of his power was now established in material control of the weaker nations of the world and would hold the economic, military and political domination of the world indefinitely.

Some such views as these were probably held by every educated person in audiences to whom 'Abdu'l-Bahá spoke in the West; more particularly by those in England; and that such views of the achievements of the Western mind prevailed twenty years or more after 'Abdu'l-Bahá's visit will be suggested by the following quotation from a famous historical work by a brilliant and illustrious Oxford scholar:

> Our civilization, then, is distinct: it is also all-pervading and preponderant. In superficial area Europe is surpassed by Asia, Africa, and America, in population by the vast stable peasantry of Asia, which outnumbers not Europe only, but the rest of the

world put together. Yet if a comprehensive survey of the globe were to be made, it would be found that in almost every quarter of it there were settlements of European men, or traces of the operation of the European mind. The surviving aboriginal peoples in the western hemisphere are a small, unimportant, and dwindling element in the population. The African negroes have been introduced by white men as an economic convenience. Northern and southern America are largely populated by colonists from Europe. Australasia is British. The political direction of Africa has fallen, with the ambiguous exception of the lower reaches of the Nile, into European hands. In Asia the case is not dissimilar. The political influences of Europe are apparent, even where they are not, as in India or Palestine, embodied in direct European control. The ideas of nationality and responsible government, of freedom and progress, of democracy and democratic education, have passed from the west to the east with revolutionary and far-reaching consequences.

It is, moreover, to European man that the world owes the incomparable gifts of modern science. To the conquest of nature through knowledge the contributions made by Asiatics have been negligible and by Africans (Egyptians excluded) non-existent. The printing press and the telescope, the steam-engine, the internal combustion engine and the aeroplane, the telegraph and telephone, wireless broadcasting and the cinematograph, the gramophone and television, together with all the leading discoveries in physiology, the circulation of the blood, the laws of respiration and the like, are the result of researches carried out by white men of European stock. It is hardly excessive to say that the material fabric of modern civilized life is the result of the intellectual daring and tenacity of the European peoples.[*]

'Abdu'l-Bahá, of course, knew that such opinions of the importance of Western civilization were utterly and cruelly illusive. He knew that the Báb had called on the peoples of the West to come forth from their cities and aid the Cause of God, warning all humanity of the *most terrible, the most grievous vengeance of God*;[†] that Bahá'u'lláh had said that the time for the destruction of the world and its people had arrived.

> *The days are approaching their end, and yet the peoples of the earth are seen sunk in grievous heedlessness, and lost in manifest error.*
>
> *Great, great is the Cause! The hour is approaching when the most great convulsion will have appeared. I swear by Him Who is the Truth! It shall cause separation to afflict every one, even those who circle around Me.*
>
> *Say, O concourse of the heedless! I swear by God! The promised day is come, the day when tormenting trials will have surged above your heads, and beneath your feet, saying: 'Taste ye what your hands have wrought!'*

---

[*] H. A. L. Fisher, *A History of Europe,* Introduction pp. 1, 2. Edward Arnold & Co., London, 1936.
[†] *Selections from the Writings of the Báb*, Chapter LIII.

The day is approaching when its [civilization's] *flame will devour the cities, when the Tongue of Grandeur will proclaim: 'The Kingdom is God's, the Almighty, the All-Praised!'*[*]

He knew that Bahá'u'lláh had declared that divine chastisement would assail the kings of the earth. He knew from the sudden doom of the Emperor Napoleon III and of the Pope, a year after the warnings given them, how sudden and terrible this retribution might be. And the Christian Bible was the accepted authority as to the coming of the Kingdom of God and of the great events that should be associated with it, and He was not likely to forget the pronouncements of horror and doom and the abasement of man's pride that according to prophets like Isaiah, Joel, Zechariah and many another were to be among the signs of the Day of the Lord. Nor would He forget how, by prophets like Ezekiel, terrible warfare and vast carnage were foretold as preceding the final victory of God on earth. He would not forget the prediction of Jesus that affliction such as the world had never known would precede that victory and that no flesh would be saved unless the time were shortened. In the book of *Revelation* the hosts of righteousness are shown as being led by Christ against the hosts of evil and the awfulness of the bloodshed that would ensue is dramatically portrayed by pictures of the wine vats flowing blood-red with the blood of the grapes.

All these Bible prophecies agreed in large and in little with the events that were now taking shape

---

[*] Bahá'u'lláh quoted in *The Advent of Divine Justice*, p. 89.

through the Word of Bahá'u'lláh, and were in utter contrast with the character and the outlook of history as the people of the West saw them. God's Will was the ruling force in the Bible as man's will dominates the direction of events in the Western mind.

It would have been easy and natural for 'Abdu'l-Bahá in the circumstances to have challenged the Western fallacy, exposed its error, developed an argument brilliant and overpowering to emphasize the agreement of His teaching with that of the Bible, and the hollowness of the Western expectation of a man-made kingdom and of materialistic hegemony of one race over others. But 'Abdu'l-Bahá did nothing of the kind. The great ideal which He held before His audiences was at all times and places one and the same: Unity Through Love. His *Paris Talks* are full throughout of a spiritual wisdom; a spontaneous warmth of heart and sweetness and winning tenderness that would be hard to match in the world's revealed religious literature. His first public address was delivered in a Christian Church in London[*]. He said,

> *This is a new cycle of human power. All the horizons of the world are luminous, and the world will become indeed as a garden and a paradise . . . The gift of God to this enlightened age is the knowledge of the oneness of mankind and of the fundamental oneness of religion. Wars shall cease between nations, and by the will of God the Most Great Peace shall come.*[†]

---

[*] City Temple, 15 September 1911.
[†] *'Abdu'l-Bahá in London*, p. 19.

This truth of a new dawning of power in the world became the master thought of all His speeches throughout His work in the West. In America, however, He addressed the Americans particularly as Christians and made an appeal to them not to be listeners only but to become the reapers whom Christ had prophesied would arise in His harvest day. He sought not only to instruct and illumine the minds of His audience but to awaken in them the power of spirituality and enthusiasm which would overcome the materialism that infected mankind and would develop in them a new loving spirituality which would enable His message to get home to their hearts.

He presented a new picture of Christ in contrast to the Christ of orthodoxy, of sect and schism and dogma; one which showed that Christ's real purpose was to unite human hearts with the power of Divine love; such a Christ as none had really conceived, eager, vigorous, bringing together people of all sorts and kinds and races and nations and overwhelming the prejudices and traditions which separated them. The natural force of His own warm, buoyant, loving nature gave power and reality to His presentation so that He was able to reveal a new Christ such as the people had never realized.

His American addresses open on a note of joy, of spontaneous abounding happiness and gratification at His meeting so many radiant hearts ready to listen to the Message which, in spite of His old age and imperfect health, He had come so far to give them. Only love from God and them would have brought Him. Heart and soul 'Abdu'l-Bahá radiated a triumphant confidence, clear and strong as can be, as He extolled the glory of Christ and Bahá'u'lláh, showing their closeness, the unity of their effort and their purpose.

His appeal was not to authority as was that of Bahá'u'lláh addressing the kings. He did not command. His appeal rather was to reason, to logic, to faith and to facts. He exposed the false hopes of the arrogant white race, not by disproof but by drawing in a quite natural manner a picture of the true antecedents of the Kingdom, showing it to be involved in the original creation of man.

He drew, in many aspects, a picture of the whole universe as governed by one unchanging law, as being created, ruled over and directed by one universal, independent, living Will. This great, out-working Spirit actuated the affairs and movements of all creatures in the world; it was the one Power which animated and dominated all existence. 'Abdu'l-Bahá spoke on this subject in an attitude of soul as logical as it was religious, as much in the mood of science as of faith. He treated the subject not only in a broad and general manner but in close detail. He traced, for example, the coursing of the atom through the kingdoms of nature – mineral, vegetable and animal – showing the changes that it assumes in its progress, through an activity not originating by itself. He showed that the one, living, independent Will of God which directed the transition of the atom directed likewise the movements which led mankind from one stage to another on its journey to the Kingdom. Thus He brought all nature into the same plane as man and showed, not only the oneness of mankind but of the whole universe – everything contributing, each in its own way – even if it be a preparatory way – towards the one great spiritual goal shown at its highest in the Kingdom of God.

He taught His auditors to meet the materialism of the day with reason and hard facts and He gave them Himself examples of how it could be done.

'Abdu'l-Bahá's first aim in His Western teaching was, as He says Himself, to create in the minds of His hearers capacity to understand and appreciate this great new Revelation. He did not wish them to be as the kings had shown themselves to be, so infected by the pride of man and the haughty scepticism of the age that they could not see the truth when it was put plainly and clearly before them. Christ, He reminded His auditors, had had the same difficulty and had spoken the parable of the sower to show it. 'Abdu'l-Bahá sought, as Christ in His day had done, to transform and spiritualize the very hearts and outlook of those to whom He spoke. Unless He could do this the exposure of one error in the minds of the people would only be followed on the next occasion by another error. No remedy was adequate except that of creating a real capacity in the human heart to see and love the truth. This and nothing less was the first and last aim of 'Abdu'l-Bahá.

His own personality was His greatest argument: He was so utterly sincere, so full Himself of truth and love that He had the power to convince (it would seem) even the most faithless.

In the second place His happy joyous way of presenting the argument appealed to those He spoke to and has its own penetrating power.

Those who knew 'Abdu'l-Bahá would say they

could feel His overflowing love for mankind pouring from Him in great waves, and some have told how to sit beside Him in a motor-car was to feel oneself being charged by spiritual energy. What strikes many in reading His writings is that they possess a quality different from that which belongs to any human being. There is a cadence, a power in them which definitely comes from a higher world than that in which we live. It is natural, therefore, that His writings should be spoken of as Revelation. Yet He was human, not a Manifestation, and His scripture, though valid, has not the rank of the Revelation of a full Prophet. What explanation can there be of this except that the Holy Spirit is now in this Age of Truth touching men's souls with a higher degree of power than ever in the past. Our age has risen from the levels of the Kingdom of Man to the heights unapproached before of the Kingdom of God. 'Abdu'l-Bahá, the embodiment of every Bahá'í ideal, the incarnation of every Bahá'í virtue, presents man (revealed as made in the image of God) at a level higher than any we associate with man before.

Completing His Western tours, 'Abdu'l-Bahá, after nine months' ceaseless lecturing in the United States and Canada, reluctantly announced the imminent outbreak of the First World War and then went by Europe back to His home in Haifa. He had, however, published translations of a number of Bahá'í Scriptures in America; organized Bahá'í communities in that country on a firm foundation; laid the foundation stone of a Bahá'í Temple in Wilmette on a site purchased at His direction. His efforts, however, to spread the Glad Tidings of the new Day far and wide found all too little response. After the outbreak of the First World War He tried to take the fullest advantage of the horror of war which the carnage had aroused by writing in and after 1916, a stirring summons to all Bahá'ís to arouse themselves and go forth through the length and breadth of the world to call all nations to the Kingdom of God. Once more He quoted the wonderful examples of the Apostles of Christ as a challenge to self-sacrifice. Fourteen of these letters constitute 'Abdu'l-Bahá's Divine Plan in which He detailed a vigorous and forthright programme for the carrying of the message of the New Day throughout the continents and the islands of the sea – a plan fully worked out and likely to be in use for many generations to come. No great response was aroused among the Bahá'ís by this appeal, a fact which caused 'Abdu'l-Bahá poignant sorrow, compelling Him to realize how deep the suffering of the world would be which all His efforts had not been able to mitigate. Broken in heart He passed to His end three years after the War, foretelling that another war, fiercer than the last, would follow before long.

On His death the most deeply conceived and constructive of His works was published, known as *The Will and Testament of 'Abdul-Bahá*. It completed the great masterpiece of Bahá'u'lláh – His book of laws* – the two works together composing one complete and harmonious whole.

---

* *Kitáb-i-Aqdas*

A STUDY OF A CHRISTLIKE CHARACTER

This essay was first published in the *Church of Ireland Gazette* in 1935, was reprinted in *World Order*, October 1936, issued in pamphlet form together with George Townshend's *Reflection on the Hidden Words of Bahá'u'lláh*, included in a compilation of his essays and has been widely used throughout the Bahá'í world. It develops a thought of the Reverend Canon T. K. Cheyne, the distinguished 'higher critic': 'No one, so far as my observation reaches, has lived the perfect life like 'Abdu'l-Bahá.' Professor Cheyne, in a letter to John Craven, an early English Bahá'í, wrote: 'Why I am a Bahá'í is a larger question, but the perfection of the characters of Bahá'u'lláh and 'Abdu'l-Bahá is perhaps the chief reason.'

To live today in deed and truth the kind of life that Jesus of Nazareth lived and bade His followers lead; to love God wholeheartedly and for God's sake to love all mankind, even one's slanderers and enemies; to give consistently good for evil, blessings for curses, kindness for cruelty and, through a career darkened along its entire length by tragic misrepresentation and persecution, to preserve one's courage, one's sweetness and calm faith in God – to do all this and yet to play the man in the world of men, sharing at home and in business the common life of humanity, administering when occasion arose affairs large and small and handling complex situations with foresight and firmness – to live in such a manner throughout a long and arduous life, and, when in the fullness of time death came, to leave to multitudes of mourners a sense of desolation and to be remembered and loved by them all as the Servant of God – to how many men is such an achievement given as it has been given in this age of ours to 'Abdu'l-Bahá?

To the historian, the psychologist, the student of comparative religion, the narrative in all its aspects has much to offer of interest and value. But to the would-be Christian of the twentieth century the personal life and character of Sir Abbas Effendi make a direct and peculiar appeal.

An ordinary man who has set himself really to follow the precepts of Christ finds himself in special difficulties today. The very understanding and knowledge of the will of Christ, as well as the performance of it, seem now less easy to attain than they were for our forefathers. The accuracy of the Gospel record not only in phrase and detail but in larger matters likewise is, however unjustifiably, questioned by an increasing number of scholars. The record in any case is brief and fragmentary; and the utterances attributed to the Christ are not only very few but so terse and epigrammatic that their bearing is often uncertain and they admit of diverse interpretations. The problems of the contemporary world too are so much more complex than those of the period in which Christ lived that His words which suited so well the conditions of the past are difficult to apply to the present. Those who profess themselves the teachers of Christendom speak, as a whole, with such different voices and offer such contradictory advice that there is much bewilderment.

Guidance from both the ancient book and from living example seems, therefore, to the man in the street less easy to gain than it was once. And the natural weakness of our nature which finds so arduous the moral life demanded by Christ is no longer supported by custom and general opinion, but is, on the contrary, unhappily enervated by the influence of a self-willed and flippant age.

In the story of 'Abdu'l-Bahá the Christian comes upon something which he ardently desires and which he finds it difficult to obtain elsewhere. There awaits him here reassurance that the moral precepts of Christ are to be accepted exactly and in their entirety, that they can be lived out as fully under modern conditions as under any other, and that the highest spirituality is quite compatible with sound common sense and practical wisdom. Many of the incidents in 'Abdu'l-Bahá's life form a commentary on the teachings of Christ and dramatise the meaning of the ancient words. Being a philosopher as well as a saint, He was able to give to many a Christian enquirer explanations of the Gospel-ideal which had the simple authority both of His consistent life and of their own reasonableness.

Christ taught that the supreme human achievement is not any particular deed nor even any particular condition of mind: but a relation to God. To be completely filled – heart, mind, soul – with love for God, such is the great ideal, the Great Commandment. In 'Abdu'l-Bahá's character the dominant element was spirituality. Whatever was good in His life He attributed not to any separate source of virtue in Himself but to the power and beneficence of God. His single aim was servitude to God. He rejoiced in being denuded of all earthly possessions and in being rich only in His love for God. He surrendered His freedom that He might become the bond-servant of God; and was able, at the close of His days, to declare that He had spent all His strength upon the Cause of God.

To Him God was the centre of all existence here on earth as heretofore and hereafter. All things were in their degree mirrors of the bounty of God and outpourings of His power. Truth was the word of God. Art was the worship of God. Life was nearness to God; death remoteness from Him. The knowledge of God was the purpose of human existence and the summit of human attainment. No learning nor education that did not lead towards this knowledge was worth pursuit. Beyond it there was no further glory, and short of it there was nothing that could be called success.

In 'Abdu'l-Bahá this love for God was the ground and cause of an equanimity which no circumstance could shake and of an inner happiness which no adversity affected and which (it is said) in His presence brought to the sad, the lonely or the doubting the most precious companionship and healing. He had many griefs but they were born of His sympathy and His devotion. He knew many sorrows, but they were all those of a lover. Warmly emotional as He was He felt keenly the troubles of others, even of persons whom He had not actually met nor seen, and to His tender and responsive nature the loss of friends and the bereavements of which He had to face more than a few brought acute anguish. His heart was burdened always with the sense of humanity's orphanhood, and He would be so much distressed by any unkindness or discord among believers that His physical health would be affected. Yet He bore His own sufferings, however numerous and great, with unbroken strength. For forty years He endured in a Turkish prison rigours which would have killed most men in a twelvemonth. Through all this time He was, He said, supremely happy, being close to God and in constant communion with Him. He made light of all His afflictions. Once, when He was paraded through the streets in chains the soldiers, who had become His friends, wished to cover up His fetters with the folds of His garment that the populace might not see and deride, but the prisoner shook off the covering and jangled aloud the bonds which He bore in the service of His Lord. When friends from foreign lands visited Him in prison and, seeing the cruelties to which He was subjected, commiserated with Him, He disclaimed their sympathy, demanded their felicitations and bade them become so firm in their love for God that they, too, could endure calamity with a radiant acquiescence. He was not really, He said, in prison; for *there is no prison but the prison of self*, and since God's love filled His heart He was all the time in heaven.

From this engrossing love for God came the austere simplicity which marked 'Abdu'l-Bahá's character. Christ's manner of life had been simple in the extreme. A poor man, poorly clad, often in His wanderings He had no drink but the running stream, no bed but the earth, no lamp but the stars. His teaching was given in homely phrases and familiar images, and the religion He revealed, however difficult to follow, was as plain and open as His life. His very simplicity helped to mislead His contemporaries. They could recognise the badges of greatness but not greatness itself, and they could not see light though they knew its name. He was neither Rabbi nor Shaykh, though He was the Messiah. He had neither throne nor sword, though all things in heaven and in earth were committed into His charge.

The life of 'Abdu'l-Bahá, too, was simple and severe. Familiar during much of His life with cold, hunger and all privation, He chose for Himself in His own home the most frugal fare. The room in which He slept (sometimes denying Himself even the comfort of a bed!) served Him as a workroom too. His clothing was often of the cheapest kind; and He taught His family so to dress that their apparel might be *an example to the rich and an encouragement to the poor*. The household prayers which He held morning and evening were quite informal.

Partly from a natural modesty but also from a resolve to do nothing that might encourage in others a tendency to formalism, He objected to any parade or unnecessary ceremonial, particularly if He were to be concerned in it.

Even if some degree of circumstance and formality were called for, He would reduce to the smallest possible proportions. When, on April 17th, 1921, He was to receive from Lord Allenby in the grounds of the Governor's Residence at Haifa the honour of knighthood for services rendered to the people of Palestine during the Turkish occupation, He evaded the equestrian procession and the military reception prepared for Him, by slipping unobserved from His house and making His way to the rendezvous by some unaccustomed route. When all were in perplexity and many thought that He was lost, He appeared quietly at the right place and the right time and proceeded in the prescribed manner with the essential part of the ceremony.

Of all material things, as of food, clothing, shelter, He sought and desired for Himself the barest sufficiency. But asceticism was not part of His creed nor of His teaching. *Others may sleep on soft pillows; mine must be a hard one*, He said once in declining a kind friend's offer of some little comfort for His room. Men were to take what God had given them, and to enjoy the good things of nature; but with renunciation. Fasting was a symbol, and as such had high value, but in itself was no virtue: *God has given you an appetite*, He said; *eat*. Riches He thought no blessing; if they had been Christ would have been rich. The poverty, however, which He inculcated was not impecuniousness but the heart's poverty of him who is so rich in love for God that He is destitute of all desire for aught else.

He was the most unassuming of men. He counted Himself personally as less than others, put Himself below them and served them in every way He could find with unaffected humility. He used to entertain at His table visitors from far and near; but if the occasion were one of special importance He would rise and wait on His guests with His own hands – a practice He recommended to other hosts.

When His father was alive and dwelt outside 'Akká in view of the mountains, 'Abdu'l-Bahá used frequently to visit Him, and though the way was long He habitually went on foot. His friends asked Him why He did not spare Himself so much time and effort and go on horseback. *Over these mountains Jesus walked on foot*, He said, *and who am I that I should ride where the Lord Christ walked?*

But this humility did not come from any weakness. It was a proof of His strength and a cause of His spiritual power. Once when a child asked Him why all the rivers of the earth flowed into the ocean, be said: *Because it sets itself lower than them all and so draws them to itself.* Pride repels; humility attracts. When commenting on Christ's direction to be as little children, He emphasised the fact that the virtues of children are due to weakness, and adults must learn to have these virtues through strength. A palsied arm cannot strike an angry blow; but the virtue of forbearance belongs to one who can but will not. His humility was not due to any diffidence or other failing. Nor did it imply any self-abasement or self-depreciation. What it meant was the obliteration of the personal self. His separate ego had no existence at all save only as an instrument of expression for the higher self that was one with God.

Somebody who knew Him in the West remarked that He was always master of the situation, and amid the novel and alien surroundings of such cities as London, Chicago and New York He preserved His self-possession and His power. On one occasion in America, when He had arrived at a house where He was to be a guest at luncheon, a coloured man called on Him just before the meal hour. Being known to the hostess the caller was admitted, but 'Abdu'l-Bahá observed that, according to the prevailing social custom, there was no intention of admitting him to sit at the table with the regular guests. Now race prejudice is what 'Abdu'l-Bahá could not tolerate. At His own table members of all races and religions met on an equality as brothers. He was not going to countenance it among His friends in America if He could help it. What was the surprise of the hostess and of everyone else present when He was observed clearing a place beside Him and calling for knives and forks for the new arrival! Before any seemly way of countering 'Abdu'l-Bahá's initiative was found, before anyone had quite realized how it had happened, the lady found herself doing what neither she nor any other hostess in her position would have dreamed of doing, and entertaining at her table with her white friends a negro. 'Abdu'l-Bahá had become the spiritual host. He spread before those who sat with Him the reality of the Fatherhood of God. Such was His radiant power that the unconventional challenging meal passed off without unpleasantness or embarrassment to any who partook of it.

When He was travelling in the West it was His custom to take out with Him a bag of silver pieces to give to the poor whom He met; and being brought down one evening to the Bowery Mission in New York He delivered there one of the most compassionate and moving of His addresses. It reads in part as follows:

Tonight I am very happy for I have come here to meet my friends. I consider you my relatives, my companions, and I am your comrade. You must be thankful to God that you are poor, for His Holiness Jesus Christ has said: 'Blessed are the poor.' He never said, 'Blessed are the rich.' He said, too, that the Kingdom is for the poor. Therefore you must be thankful to God that though in this world you are indigent yet the treasures of God are within your reach; and although in the material realm you are poor, yet in the Kingdom of God you are precious. His Holiness Jesus Himself was poor. He did not belong to the rich. He passed His time in the desert travelling among the poor, and lived upon the herbs of the field. He had no place to lay His head, no home; yet He chose this rather than riches. It was the poor who accepted Him first, not the rich. Therefore you are the disciples of Jesus; you are His comrades; your lives are similar to His life, your attitude is like unto His, you resemble Him more than the rich. Therefore we will thank God that we have been so blest with real riches and, in conclusion, I ask you to accept 'Abdu'l-Bahá as your servant.

At the end of the meeting 'Abdu'l-Bahá stood at the Bowery entrance to the Mission Hall shaking hands with from four to five hundred men and placing within each palm a piece of silver.

With no less tenderness He answered the need of those whose poverty was spiritual. His guards and jailers, servants of a cruel and despotic master, were won by His kindness and became His friends. 'What is there about Him,' people would say, 'that He makes His enemies His friends?'

Towards those who displayed to Him personal ill-will and malice He showed forbearance and generosity. Missionary work, He said, is not promoted by being overbearing and harsh; bad people are not to be won to God by criticisms and rebukes, nor by returning to them evil for evil. On the contrary, the Cause of God advances through courtesy and kindness, and the bad are conquered by intercession on their behalf and by sincere, unflagging love. *When you meet a thought of hate overcome it with a stronger thought of love.*

Christ's command to love one's enemies was not obeyed by assuming Love nor by acting as though one loved them; for this would be hypocrisy. It was only obeyed when genuine love was felt. When asked how it was possible to love those who were hostile or personally repugnant, He said that love could be true yet indirect. One may love a flower not only for itself but for the sake of someone who sent it. One may love a house because of one who dwells in it. A letter coming from a friend may be precious though the envelope which held it was torn and soiled. So one may love sinners for the sake of the universal Father, and may show kindness to them as to children who need training, to sick persons who need medicine, to wanderers who need guidance.

Treat the sinners, the tyrants, the bloodthirsty enemies as faithful friends and confidants, He would say. *Consider not their deeds; consider only God.* His kindness was persistent and unflagging; He forgave until seventy times seven. A neighbour of His in Haifa, a self-righteous Muslim from Afghanistan, who regarded 'Abdu'l-Bahá as a renegade and an outcast, pursued Him for years with hate and scorn. When he met 'Abdu'l-Bahá on the street he would draw aside his robes that he might not be contaminated by touching a heretic. He received kindnesses with obdurate ill will. Help in misfortune, food when he was hungry, medicine in sickness, the services of a physician, personal visits, all made no impression on his hardened heart. But 'Abdu'l-Bahá did not relax nor despair. For five and twenty years He returned continuously good for evil; and then suddenly the man's long hate broke down, his heart warmed, his spirit awoke and with tears of disillusion and remorse he bowed in homage before the goodness that had mastered him.

Even with enemies much more dangerous and cruel than this poor Afghan, 'Abdu'l-Bahá showed the same forbearance and goodwill. He would suffer or invite any personal loss or humiliation rather than miss an opportunity of doing a kindness to an enemy; He would suffer calamity in order to avoid doing something which might be to the spiritual detriment of an ill-wisher. When 'Abdu'l-Bahá had been liberated, the misrepresentations of a secret enemy resulted in His re-imprisonment. He might probably have secured His release by a special appeal; but He declined to take this action. He went back to the prison and was held there for years, one reason for this non-resistance to evil being that the success of His appeal would but deepen the envy and degradation of His enemy: *He must know that I will be the first to forgive him.* In this submissiveness He acted in the same spirit as His father in parallel circumstances. For during that period when a certain jealous member of their entourage was by various means covertly seeking His life, Bahá'u'lláh and all the members of His family, including His eldest son, remained (so Professor Cheyne records) on cordial relations with him, admitting him as before to their company, even though they thus afforded him further opportunities of pursuing his deadly designs.

So confident were all who knew 'Abdu'l-Bahá that they could count on His largeness of mind that even the Sháh of Persia, when in extremity and threatened with revolution, stooped to ask the advice of the man he had kept in prison for a lifetime, and received an assurance that if he would end despotism and establish a constitution he might count on a happy reign, but that if he persisted in his present path he would be dethroned. The Sháh neglected the counsel and brought down upon himself the fate from which his generous prisoner would have shielded him.

From His foot one may reconstruct Hercules, and from a few words and incidents one may reconstruct a character. 'Abdu'l-Bahá is no churchman; yet His qualities clarify the Christian ideal of manhood and help to prove for those who need such proof, how that ideal applies to modern as truly as to ancient conditions of life and is no less within the reach of active men today than it was in simpler times gone by.

THE LETTERS OF
'ABDU'L-BAHÁ

The first books of Bahá'í scripture which came into George Townshend's hands (July 1919) were the three volumes of *Tablets of 'Abdu'l-Bahá* (letters to early believers in North America) and the compilation of His addresses throughout the United States and Canada, published under the title *The Promulgation of Universal Peace*. Although in the following essay the addresses are mentioned, the main concern is the Tablets. It is not known when it was written, but it was first published in a compilation of some of George Townshend's works entitled *The Mission of Bahá'u'lláh* (Oxford: George Ronald, 1952).

These tablets are a fountain of heavenly love and joy, of wisdom and power. In every volume, the ceaseless, the boundless Love of God pours forth like wine into a thousand different vessels: changing its form, taking the shape of many occasions, filling exactly many needs, but never changing the exquisiteness of its beauty. Love, spontaneous and unstinted, floods every utterance of thought. There is no check, no limit. The days when these letters were written were early days, the days of the first meetings of Lovers and Beloved, the days of God's welcome to the first believers of the western world.

This is the time of happiness, the day of rejoicing and of delight (p. 320).* *With a heart overflowing with the love of God, pray to God in all joy and give Him thanks for this guidance this high gift. Could those who receive these letters but realise the joy with which they are written, they would lift up their hearts and in spirit soar heavenward in exaltation,* He writes. 'Abdu'l-Bahá at the time of writing these letters was in prison. He was misrepresented, humiliated, frustrated; His life was in danger; difficulties had to be met every hour. Yet no personal distress affects for a moment in the least degree His inward peace of heart or weakens the delight of His fellowship with those who begin to share His love for God.

Whatever sorrow there be in these pages is not for

---

* Page numbers refer to *Tablets of Abdul-Baha Abbas*, New York, Chicago, 1909–16.

Himself but is through the intensity of His sympathy with the griefs of those to whom He writes. *His heart is filled with the Love of God, is free and isolated from all save God, is illumined and overflowing with the bounties of the Kingdom of El-Abhá* (p. 713). *Verily, I am the servant of Bahá'u'lláh, the bond slave of Bahá'u'lláh, the captive of Bahá'u'lláh. I have no grade but this and I do not possess anything for myself* (p. 603).

A power from on high animates Him: the Holy Spirit moves His limbs, His pen. To suffer for God's sake to drink the cup of sacrifice is His *utmost hope, the joy of my heart, the consolation of my soul and my final desire.*

Again and again He rejects commiseration offered on account of His calamities and afflictions. *They are not calamities, but bounties, they are not afflictions but gifts; not hardships, but tranquillity; not trouble, but mercy; and we thank God for this great favour* (p. 128). He asserts His independence of all His enemies can do to harm Him.

I am free, He writes, *though I should remain in prison; all fortresses and castles cannot confine me, and the dungeon cannot bring me under the narrow bondage of the world. The spirit is ever soaring, even if the body be in the depths . . . Therefore, neither the prison is a cause of sorrow, nor freedom from it a source of joy* (p. 151).

These letters fill hundreds of printed pages. Each correspondent is addressed by some special spiritual title chosen by 'Abdu'l-Bahá for him or for her, personally, as, *Thou Who Art Turning to the Divine Kingdom, Thou Candle of the Love of God, Thou Servant of God, Thou Opened Rose in the Garden of Abhá, Thou Who*

Art Awakened to the Cause of God, Thou Worshipper of Truth, Thou Servant of Humanity, Thou Who Art Yearning for the Glad Tidings of God.

He deals with diverse problems; answers countless questions about the past and the present, about Revelation, about Christianity, about social life, the life of the home, about marriage and children. He sets forth the cause of God and its administration. He exposes the error and the evil of the times. He comforts, counsels, commands, urges; He chants praises of God and of His faithful ones. Whatever the subject, whatever the occasion, whatever the need, the same divine might of His creative love calls into action the awakening spirit of the people of the West. His heart, He writes (p. 60), overflows with gladness and exultation as He reads the letters of the beloved of God whose eyes are enlightened by God, whose hearts and consciences are purified by knowledge and love of God and who have found peace of soul through the commemoration of God.

He remembers them at all times, prays for them every morn and eve (p. 113). *Do not think that ye are forgotten for one moment* (p. 593). *Trust thou in the love of 'Abdu'l-Bahá, for verily nothing equals it* (p. 201).

If for any reason letters do not reach Him He misses them and life and conscience do not find happiness and joy (p. 375). Yet important and dearly cherished as letters are He is in close and living touch with the faithful in spite of distance, in spite of interruption in correspondence. Time and place do not control the Spirit nor the inwardness of spiritual realities: geographical remoteness from a heavenly centre will not obscure the vision of its glory. *When the Spirit is breathed in the East its signs immediately appear in the West, and it hath a spiritual dominion which penetrates the pillars of the world* (p. 289). If the friends be firm in the cause of God and in His service, spiritual letters come down to them from the Kingdom of Abhá. Their descent is according to an eternal law; their movement is like that of wave following wave and they bear tidings of the unity of God. The love of 'Abdu'l-Bahá for His faithful friends is itself another and a special messenger between them. If a human heart be truly sensitive to the call of God, then there is stretched between its centre and the centre of the Kingdom a connection through which the spirit sends its messages. Every faithful loving heart is endued with this means of communion (pp. 287, 628).

'Abdu'l-Bahá is spiritually present with the faithful at their meetings and is their protector, *spreading His wings over them* (pp. 90, 282).

In phrase after phrase, passage after passage challenging, rigorous, profound, He tells of the transcendent unimagined imperishable splendour of the Abhá Kingdom they are entering (p. 289).

O maidservant of God! Every star hath a setting but the star of knowledge of God in the Divine heaven; every light shall darken save the light of the guidance of God, every glory shall vanish away save the glory under the shadow of the word of God (p. 129). He calls on the beloved (pp. 411–2) to seize the opportunity God's mercy offers them – *Truly I say unto you, this is a gift which neither the dominion of the world, nor all the riches of its treasuries, nor the glory of its distinguished men, can rival in this resplendent century and new age; inasmuch as crowns are transient but this is eternal and will never be taken away.*

In this material world nothing hath any result, even if it be dominion over the East and the West. But that which hath an immortal result is servitude in the Holy Threshold, service which is rendered to the Kingdom of God, and which gives guidance to all on the earth (p. 424). *O beloved of God! know ye that the world is like unto a mirage which the thirsty one thinks to be water . . . Leave it to its people and turn unto the Kingdom of your Lord, the merciful.*

He pours His blessing upon them. *Blessed are ye, O stars that shine with the light of the love of God! Blessed are ye, O lamps that burn with the fire of love of God. Blessed are ye whose hearts are drawn to the Kingdom. Glad tidings to you who are severed from all save God . . . Glad tidings to you through the gift of the Covenant . . . Rejoice . . . Be glad . . . Lift up your hearts . . . Let your eyes be solaced by the vision of the bounties of the spiritual Realm* (p. 30).

The cup of knowledge is floating over, blessed are they who drink of it deeply! . . . The gates of heaven are open, blessed are they who see. The hosts of heaven stand in battle-array – what joy to them who win the victory. The trumpet of life is sounding – how glad the ears of them that hear! (p. 621). He calls on them again and again to realise the supreme privilege which is vouchsafed them by the mercy of God, and to pour forth every kind of praise to Him for ever from grateful, happy, radiant hearts (pp. 182, 259, 413, 594, etc).

There is a note of warning, too: *The time is short,*

and the Divine Courser moves swiftly on (p. 406). To those who complain the path to the Kingdom is hard, obstacles many, difficulties severe; who are perplexed, burdened, discouraged, He says such trials are to be expected. Earthly aims are not won without effort and perseverance, and obstacles to these great spiritual attainments naturally are greater still.

Through steadfastness in overcoming these trials, the soul of the believer is brought nearer to God and at last reaches the condition of knowledge and assurance. As Nature, having borne with patience the lightning and thunderbolts and storms of winters, is afterwards rewarded with the season of blossoms, flowers and fruits; so in the Kingdom of heaven the storms of trials give a constant heart the means of earning the good pleasure of God and the prizes of the Kingdom.

How extreme in times long past were the troubles of the lovers of Christ. Yet their courage was proof, and their reward was eternal life and everlasting Glory.

If tests are severe, it is that they may expose the weakness of those who are unworthy, and enable every true hearted soul to *shine from the horizon of the Most Great Guidance.* To any such soul tests, however violent, are a gift from God, the Exalted, and He hastens towards them with joy and gladness, for they will cleanse him of those imperfections that keep him removed from his Beloved (p. 722).

'Abdu'l-Bahá bids the faithful not to be grieved at the divine trials: but to turn to God, to bow before His will in lowliness, to pray to Him, to be content under all conditions, to be thankful to Him in the midst of affliction.

They are to know that in this age the greatest of all titles, the highest of all praise is given for resolution and firmness because the tests and trials are of the greatest intensity.

The mastery of life and its trials belongs only to believers and comes only from turning to God. When asked about problems of human relationships or the life of the home He affirms that one must at all times be free from merely personal desires and warmed with devotion to God. One must love all people and one's own family with a ray of the infinite Godward love – personal love is not enough.

To one whose home was a place of strain He wrote: *It behoveth thee to sever thyself from all desires save for thy Lord the supreme, expecting no aid or help from anyone in the Universe, not even thy father or children. Resign thyself to God . . . Be patient. Endure every difficulty and hardship with an uplifted heart, an aspiring spirit, a tongue that delights to make mention of the All-merciful* (pp. 97–8). To another He wrote explaining: *When thou beholdest with the eye of truth, then thou wilt realise that in this world neither known nor unknown, neither kind father nor beloved son, neither mother nor sister help us. No persons assist except the benevolent Almighty. When thou knowest Him, thou art independent of all else. When thou art attached to His love then thou art detached kith and kin* (p. 671). Only when the heart has broken the lure of a limited love can it be attuned to the perfect love, the perfect joy that will satisfy it for ever.

Know that in every home where God is praised and prayed to, and His Kingdom proclaimed, that home is a garden of God and a paradise of His happiness (p. 69).

He writes of the importance of marriage and of its responsibilities (e.g., pp. 609, 627) and shows (p. 605) that true marriage is accessible only to the spiritually minded, and that the real bond between husband and wife is none other than the Word of God.

He suggests that the naming of a child should be made a religious and social occasion: that friends should be invited to the home and that before the name is given suitable prayers should be said; after which the company should enjoy some light repast together. He calls for obedience and kindness from children to their parents (p. 551); and on the other hand, in the strongest manner, stresses the obligation laid by God in this Dispensation on parents to bring up their children in the knowledge and fear of God. *Should they neglect this matter they shall be held responsible and worthy of reproach in the presence of the stern Lord. This is a sin unpardonable . . .* (p. 579).

For those who seek comfort in the anguish of a fresh bereavement He lifts a little the veil that hides from them that eternal world in which love knows no separation. He bids them remember this parting is limited to the body, its length will be counted in days and over the Spirit death has no dominion at all. Reunion and everlasting consolation are near. *Thy son shall be with thee in the Kingdom of God and thou shalt behold his smiling face and his brow illumined with the beauty of eternal happiness; then thou wilt have comfort and wilt give thanks to God for His loving kindness to thee* (p. 86).

To the faithful or as He names them *the people of*

adoration, He writes *death is an ark of deliverance* (p. 444). Could these mourners but see in heaven now the faithful souls they lament, wonder and joy would check their tears. He comforts a mourning mother (p. 405): *O Bird of the Rose-Garden of Fidelity! Be of no cheerless heart; have no wing nor feather broken; sigh not, neither do thou wail nor sit chilled in a corner. The little girl lamented is in the divine Rose-Garden in the highest happiness and delight. Why then art thou grieved, sorrowing with a bleeding heart? This is the day of rejoicing and the hour of ecstasy. This is the season of the spiritually dead coming forth from their graves and gathering together. This is the promised time for the attainment of plenteous grace.*

Be calm, be strong, be grateful, and become a lamp full of light, that the darkness of sorrow may be scattered and the sun of everlasting joy arise in brilliant splendour from the dawning place of heart and soul. Upon thee be the Glory of the Most Glorious!

To a physician seeking counsel, He writes: *Whenever thou presentest thyself at the bed of a patient turn thy face towards the Lord of the Kingdom and supplicate assistance from the Holy Spirit and heal the ailments of the sick one* (p. 685).

Answering an enquiry about the nature of the sympathetic nervous system He explains that the powers of the sympathetic nerve are not exclusively spiritual nor exclusively physical, but are between the two and connected with both. The operation of the nerve is normal when its relations with the spiritual and the physical systems are perfect. *When the material and the divine world are rightly co-related, when the hearts become heavenly and the aspirations grow pure and divine, then perfect connection between the two systems will follow. Then shall this power be shown in its perfection, and physical and spiritual diseases shall receive complete healing. The exposition is brief. Ponder, and thou shall understand the meaning* (p. 309).

All life in reality opens on heaven, and all experience lies in the path of God. To those who consult Him about the study and practice of letters, music, painting, science, and the like, 'Abdu'l-Bahá explains that these pursuits are one and all to be inspired by the sense of worship. *Art is worship,* as He once said. He affirms that a spiritual motive in the artist will quicken his progress and heighten his proficiency. A believer will find his art a natural medium of communicating the Divine Message; if his work has itself a spiritual quality it will awaken the spiritual susceptibilities of the beholder while his social intercourse with fellow-artists will tend to guide their thoughts to appreciation of the Divine Beauty (pp. 449–50).

At the present time all divine power poured from heaven on humanity has its focus in Bahá'u'lláh, and reaches mankind through His mediation alone. As in our solar system the source of all physical light is the sun, and every light directly or indirectly is derived from it, so in the spiritual realm every Age has its Messiah and truth is attained by men only through Him (p. 592). *Whatever question thou hast in thy heart,* writes 'Abdu'l-Bahá, *turn thou thy heart towards the kingdom of Abhá and entreat at the threshold of the Almighty and reflect upon that problem; then unquestionably the light of Truth shall dawn and the reality of that problem will become evident and clear to thee. For the teachings of His Highness Bahá'u'lláh are the keys to all the doors* (p. 692).

In the past, He points out, there were great philosophers who upheld the ideal of the oneness of humanity; but at that time the support and inspiration of heaven were not forthcoming so that their endeavours bore no fruit. Today there are many souls in the world who spread thoughts of peace and reconciliation and long to establish the unity of the human race. But they likewise are without the dynamic power to carry their ideal into effect. This power belongs only to the instructions and exhortations of Bahá'u'lláh whose summons to world-unity is supported by the word of God and by all the resources of the Kingdom of the Most High. *Therefore, O thou lover of the oneness of the world of humanity, spread thou as much as thou canst the instructions and teachings of His Highness Bahá'u'lláh* (p. 691).

There is indeed need of a thousand teachers, He writes, each one severed from the world, attracted by the Holy Spirit, radiant with the joy of the Kingdom, seeking no reward or recompense. *Strive with life and guide the people to the Kingdom of God, lead them to the straight pathway, inform them of the greatness of the Cause and give them the glad tidings* (p. 360).

The world of humanity today is like a sick and feeble man; the teachers are wise physicians. The remedies which they are to apply are two. The first to be given is that of guidance, that the people *may turn unto God, hearken to the divine commandments and go forth with a hearing ear and a seeing eye*. When this remedy has had its effect, then the people are *to be trained in the conduct, morals and deeds of the Supreme Concourse, encouraged and inspired with the gifts of the Kingdom of Abhá* (pp. 36–7). Their hearts are to be cleansed of all ill-will and to be strengthened in all the attributes of love and union so that East and West may be joined in one, and universal peace be established. In the pursuit of their task, teachers are not to spare themselves nor to seek rest. They are to make the utmost endeavour to bring the Glad Tidings to the ears of mankind and are to accept every calamity and affliction in their love for God and their reliance on 'Abdu'l-Bahá (p. 38). They are to drink from the eternal chalice of the love of God, to enjoy its ecstasy and in the radiance of the beauty of Abhá be all aglow with zeal, delight and eager energy. They all are to work together in perfect unanimity and singleness of purpose. *Ye must attain such spiritual unity and agreement that ye may express one spirit and one life* (p. 23).

It was to this end, to unite the hearts of the beloved of God, that Bahá'u'lláh endured all difficulties and all ordeals (p. 247); and the aim of 'Abdu'l-Bahá's devotion and service is the same; *that union and affection may be created among the beloved of God, nay the whole of the human world* (p. 421).

Nothing can exceed the emphasis and earnestness with which in these Tablets He appeals for concord and unity among believers. This is the vital instrument through which is to be achieved the master-objective of the Bahá'í Movement, namely the transforming of the earth into a paradise, the wide world into one home, the nations of East and West into one household. *Not until this is realised will the cause advance by any means whatsoever.* Therefore, even in those early days of the Faith when believers were very few in the West, He begins the work of organisation, urges co-operation and gatherings among the friends, the forming of committees for promoting the Cause and of what were at that time called Boards of Consultation. *The greatest means for the union and harmony of all is Spiritual Meetings. This matter is very important.* (p. 125)

Such meetings will be magnets drawing down divine strength. *Blessed are ye,* He writes to one group, *for organising the assembly of unity.* As these meetings begin to materialise, He insists that the highest degree of union and harmony must exist between them. The spiritual meeting of consultation in New York must be in the fullest accord with that in Chicago, and when a similar meeting *shall be organised in Washington, these two meetings of Chicago and New York must be in unity and harmony with that meeting.*

He watches over the constitution of these bodies, instructs that each shall have its clearly marked purpose and fit into the general scheme as an integral part of the whole, and that no spirit of exclusiveness shall be aroused such as has happened in earlier Dispensations when arrangements which *were in the beginning a means for harmony became in the end a cause of trouble* (p. 394).

He enjoins, too, the great observance of the Faith, the yearly fast from March 2nd–20th; *the Fast is a duty to be observed by all* (p. 57) – and *the Feast of Remembrance or Meeting of Faithfulness* as it was then called (p. 421).

This Feast, He writes (p. 468), *was established by His Highness The Báb, to occur once in nineteen days. Likewise the Blessed Perfection hath commanded, encouraged and reiterated it. Therefore, it hath the utmost importance. Undoubtedly you must give the greatest attention to its establishment and raise it to the highest point of importance, so that it may become continual and constant.*

He then gives directions as to the keeping of the Feast; and concludes – *If the Feast is arranged in this manner and in the way mentioned, that supper is the Lord's supper, for the result is the same result and the effect is the same effect* (pp. 468–9).

These Tablets, published in America and written chiefly to American believers, form a sister – and complementary – volume to that which contains 'Abdu'l-Bahá's American addresses and bears the title *The Promulgation of Universal Peace.* Taken together they form, as it were, a complete circle of Divine and practical instruction for the times.

The Addresses constitute the profoundest and most comprehensive textbook on modern problems. They reveal what true modernism is, dealing with the larger aspects of the Cause of Bahá'u'lláh, with questions of the relations and the history of religions and of peoples, with science and philosophy, with the principles of world order and with definite plans for its establishment. The Tablets, on the other hand, are directed for the most part to individuals, often to individuals who look to Him with ardent belief and adoring love. They reveal clearly and emphatically the essential nature of His own special station as the bondservant of Bahá'u'lláh and the Centre of the Covenant.

They are heart to heart talks on the personal hopes and aspirations of His correspondents, their personal trials and difficulties, their personal duties and obligations to God and His Faith. The writer's attitude is that of a host greeting an honoured and loved guest, a father welcoming a dear son home from a long and perilous journey: it is that of a divine messenger who brings to those struggling in the uncertain turmoil of earthly life a foretaste of the sweetness and fragrance and harmony and peace of Paradise and of the eternal glory and power that will be the reward of victory.

'Abdu'l-Bahá stated that these Tablets have an importance which will not be appreciated for many long years to come. But perhaps their message of the impassioned all-embracing love of God will never be more sadly needed than it is now, nor more precious than it is to us as we battle on through the heart of the storm and the darkness and the ruin of the Night of Judgment and Retribution.

THE FIRE OF THE KING'S LOVE

This is the title of Chapter IX of *The Promise of All Ages* already cited. Chapter VIII deals with the social and administrative aspects of God's kingdom on earth. Now the motivation of all human effort is shown by 'Abdu'l-Bahá to be love of God. Whether in the pursuit of happiness, of greater knowledge, of an ever-advancing civilisation, of individual refinement and spiritual perception, love of God is the unfailing power which will bring about the unity of mankind, solve the difficult problems of the age, heal the wounds inflicted upon the earth and its peoples and bring to realisation the age-old dream of the brotherhood of man.

Not by divine instruction, not by mind knowledge, nor by the following of a code of law or system of administration is the unification of mankind to be established or inaugurated, but rather by a true abiding love that burns away difference of self-interest, and melts by its flame all hearts into one heart. Each stands for all, and where one is all are.

Love, wrote 'Abdu'l-Bahá in one of his tablets,

> *Love is the principle of God's holy Dispensation, the Manifestation of the All-Merciful, the fountain of spiritual outpourings. Love is heaven's kindly light, the Holy Spirit's eternal breath that vivifies the human soul. Love is the cause of God's Revelation unto man, the vital bond inherent according to divine creation in the essences of things. Love is the one means that ensures true felicity both in this world and in the next. Love is the light that guides in darkness, the living link that unites God with man, that assures the progress of every illumined soul. Love is the supreme law that rules this mighty and heavenly cycle, the sole power that binds together the divine elements of this material world, the supreme magnetic force that directs the movements of the spheres in the celestial realms. Love reveals with unfailing and limitless power the mysteries latent in the universe. Love is the spirit of life within the beautified body of mankind; it establishes true civilisation in this mortal world, and sheds imperishable glory upon every aspiring race and nation ....*

He extolled the power created within man by this love for God.

> *By the fire of the Love of God the veil is burned which separates us from the Heavenly Realities, and with clear vision we are enabled to struggle onward and upward, ever progressing in the paths of virtue and holiness, and becoming the means of light to the world. There is nothing greater or more blessed than love for God. It gives healing to the sick, balm to the wounded, joy and consolation to the whole world, and through it alone can man attain Life Everlasting. The Essence of all religions is the love for God, and it is the foundation of all the sacred teachings* (Paris Talks, p. 74).

There are on earth many semblances and many mockeries of the high name of love; but authentic love is rare. A worldly friend, Bahá'u'lláh taught, in his love for others is really thinking of himself and his own good; his love is unreal. *Whereas the true friend hath loved and doth love you for your own sakes; indeed he hath suffered for your guidance countless afflictions* (*Hidden Words*, Persian no. 52).

'Abdu'l-Bahá would warn His hearers against putting their trust in a love that was not of the truest. He uttered in His gentle way warnings against a love that was mere fascination, a love that was based (however subtly) on self-interest, a love that had its end in antipathy and hate. A love that has its selfishness or its limits is not enough. True love in no way seeks its own, nor counts its gifts, and God in this age demands from His creatures both for Himself and for one another the truth and very reality of love.

* * * * *

In one of his talks in Paris, 'Abdu'l-Bahá emphasised the boundlessness of true love, and affirmed that now through the gift of the Holy Spirit such love was brought within reach of the sons of men. Love of family, of nation, of race, of party, these and such limited expressions of love were all inadequate.

The great unselfish love for Humanity, He said, *is bounded by none of these imperfect semi-selfish bonds; this is the one perfect Love, possible to all mankind, and it can only be achieved by the Power of the Holy Spirit. No worldly power can accomplish this universal love* (*Paris Talks*, p. 32).

No provocation is admitted by God as an excuse for a Bahá'í's lack of love. Lovingkindness is to be a constant impregnable attitude of soul.

The more they oppose thee, wrote 'Abdu'l-Bahá to one whose patience was sorely tried, *the more do thou shower upon them justice and equity. The more they show hatred and opposition, the more do thou challenge them with truthfulness, friendship and reconciliation* (*Tablets*, pp. 557–8).

In another letter (II, 389) He explained that according to the teachings of Bahá'u'lláh believers must in this present age be the friends of all nations and of all communities. They must not let their eyes dwell upon the violence, the ill will, the persecution or the hostility that might surround them but instead should lift their gaze to the realm of divine glory and look upon these ill-doers as creatures of God, *signs of the Lord of signs* who had been brought into existence by the divine favour and volition, and were therefore to be regarded, not as strangers or aliens, but as acquaintances and friends. The believer was not to consider the merits and capabilities of people, but to show sympathy to strangers as well as to friends, to display genuine love to others under all conditions, never allowing that love to be over-borne by people's hatred, malice, contentiousness or spite. If he be made a target for their arrows, he is to give milk and honey in return; if they administer poison, he is to bestow sweetmeats; if they inflict pain, he is to answer with balm.

Love and faithfulness, He wrote (p. 125), *must so fill the heart that men will look on the stranger as a friend, . . . count enemies as allies, foes as loving comrades, their executioner as a giver of life, the denier as a believer, and the unbeliever as one of the faithful.*

Throughout the teachings this command that the heart shall be taught and the actions shall express the law of universal love is set forth repeatedly and insistently, in all its details and in all its aspects. In that sketch of the good life, for example, which 'Abdu'l-Bahá gave, and which has become the viaticum of every Bahá'í, nearly every injunction is some application of the supreme principle of love.

To live the life is:

To be no cause of grief to anyone.
   To be kind to all people and to love them with a pure spirit.

Should opposition or injury happen to us, to bear it, to be as kind as ever we can be, and through all, to love the people. Should calamity exist in the greatest degree, to rejoice, for these things are the gifts and favours of God.

To be silent concerning the faults of others, to pray for them, and to help them, through kindness, to correct their faults.

To look always at the good and not at the bad. If a man has ten good qualities and one bad one, look at the ten and forget the one. And if a man has ten bad qualities and one good one, to look at the one and forget the ten.

Never to allow ourselves to speak one unkind word about another, even though that other be our enemy.

To do all of our deeds in kindness.

To sever our hearts from ourselves and from the world.

To be humble.

To be servants of each other, and to know that we are less than anyone else.

To be as one soul in many bodies; for the more we love each other, the nearer we shall be to God; but to know that our love, our unity, our obedience must not be by confession, but of reality.

To act with cautiousness and wisdom.

To be truthful.

To be hospitable.

To be reverent.

To be a cause of healing for every sick one, a comforter for every sorrowful one, a pleasant water for every thirsty one, a heavenly table for every hungry one, a star to every horizon, a light for every lamp, a herald to everyone who yearns for the kingdom of God.

* * * * *

Such is the love that God has breathed upon the dead heart of the world. Such is the love which is to reawaken the souls of men to the consciousness of heavenly things and to quicken their spirits to a higher life. . .

This love now pouring down from God in fullest measure upon the awakening consciousness of mankind is the power that will regenerate human nature, and will create in deed and in fact a new heaven and a new earth.

FURTHER READING

Earl Redman's trilogy about 'Abdu'l-Bahá as seen through the eyes of the pilgrims and other visitors to 'Akká and Haifa and those who met Him in Europe and America. Volume 1 of *Visiting 'Abdu'l-Bahá* covers the years from 1897 to 1911. 'Abdu'l-Bahá's travels between 1910 and 1913 are described in *'Abdu'l-Bahá in Their Midst*. Volume 2 of *Visiting 'Abdu'l-Bahá* volume begins with the Master's return to Haifa in 1913 and ends with His passing in 1921.

The books are based largely on the notes of pilgrims and others who visited the Master. As such, they must be viewed simply as personal impressions, but impressions 'of a most precious character'. Those who had the privilege of meeting 'Abdu'l-Bahá carried these impressions with them until the end of their lives, and their pen-pictures have become an inspiration to many, both believers and the general public, in the century since His passing.

'Abdu'l-Baha, The Centre Of The Covenant was the first comprehensive biography of this 'magnetic figure' and 'perfect Exemplar' of Bahá'í life, and remains the foremost source for subsequent accounts.

Over 250 pages describe 'Abdu'l-Bahá's journey to the West, the places He visited and audiences He addressed, many of those who were privileged to meet him, and the example He gave in daily life. The ideals He upheld for all are reflected in a wealth of quotations from His talks.

H. M. Balyuzi, loved and honoured throughout the Bahá'í world for his invaluable books on the three Central Figures of the Bahá'í Faith, as well as for other important works, was mourned by the Universal House of Justice on his death in 1980 as one of the 'most powerful defenders, most resourceful historians' of the Faith.

Vignettes from the Life of 'Abdu'l-Bahá is a unique collection of stories, sayings and comments, providing a special insight into the life, character and station of Bahá'u'lláh's eldest son. He was universally known to Bahá'ís as the Master but wished only to be known as the Servant. Not only those qualities for which He was chosen as the Centre of Bahá'u'lláh's Covenant, but also the human virtues which made Him the Perfect Exemplar for all Bahá'ís, are amply illustrated in over two hundred and fifty vignettes of His life, drawn from a very wide range of published, out-of-print and unpublished sources. The book is divided into three main sections, *His Pure Heart, His Kindly Heart,* and *His Radiant Heart*; and for those not already acquainted with the main events of His life, there is a brief factual introduction. The book is enhanced by a mixed selection of rare and well-loved photographs, and is itself dedicated to 'Abdu'l-Bahá.

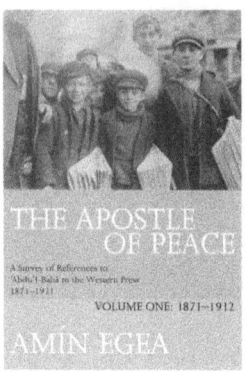 

A fascinating collection of a few hundred of the over 2,200 press articles written about 'Abdu'l-Bahá during His lifetime compiled by Amín Egea.

In an era when the newspaper was the main source of news, 'Abdu'l-Bahá gave interviews in almost every city He visited, granted press conferences and even agreed to have His picture taken. His message of peace, brotherhood and the advent of Bahá'u'lláh excited the interest of thousands and the press promulgated these ideas enthusiastically, exhibiting a genuine interest for the Master both as a religious figure and as a promulgator of progressive ideals.

The large number of articles written about Him demonstrates that He was far better known by the public than previously thought.

The first of the two volumes, covers the period 1871 to December 1912 and includes 'Abdu'l-Bahá's first visit to Europe and His journey across North America, the second from 13 December 1912 to the passing of 'Abdu'l-Bahá in November 1921, including the many articles published afterwards.

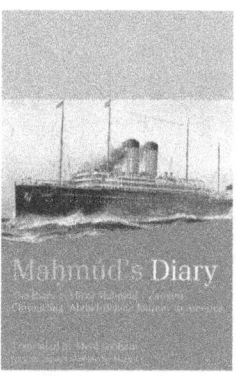

In the spring of 1912 'Abdu'l-Bahá set off from Alexandria on His historic journey to America. Among his small entourage was Mírzá Mahmúd-i-Zarqání, who became, in the words of Shoghi Effendi, 'the chronicler of His travels'.

Mírzá Mahmúd went everywhere with 'Abdu'l-Bahá, making extensive notes not only of the Master's many public talks and conversations with individuals but also of the new sights and experiences they found in America as well as the daily routines of eating, writing letters and travelling.

Mahmúd remarks on the novelty of the New York skyscrapers, electric lights and American foods and customs for 'Abdu'l-Bahá's party as well as the picturesque spectacle provided to the Americans by His entourage in their 'abás and Persian hats.

The result was a unique diary 'regarded as a reliable account of 'Abdu'l-Bahá's travels in the West and an authentic record of His utterances, whether in the form of formal talks, table talks or random oral statements.

www.ingramcontent.com/pod-product-compliance
Lightning Source LLC
Chambersburg PA
CBHW051709040426
42446CB00008B/798